Endorsements

You hold here in your hand a gift – the very transparent story of a long difficult "journey" that my friends Chuck and Evelyn Rudolph have chosen to share with all of us: a tangible demonstration of their wholehearted trust in God, no matter the outcome. Chuck has survived several reoccurrences of stage 4 cancer by God's grace, great medical care, and a personal desire to not give up. Chuck and Evelyn are my heroes. Their faith and tenacity are simply remarkable. I trust their story will encourage you as it has me – to keep our eyes on Jesus, no matter what might come our way.

Bill Shewan, Legacy Planning Advisor
Office of the President, Youth for Christ USA

This book is more than a story of one man's successful and on-going battle against cancer, Chuck Rudolph gives the reader hope when life seems the darkest and when the pain is more than you can stand. He also shares practical ways by which you can help those that are extremely sick, lonely, friendless or helpless.

Chuck has simply given you the basics on how you can survive the worst that life can throw at you. He also gives simple but effective suggestions on how you can do what Jesus did in helping others.

Dr. Ernie Taylor, Founder, VisionTrust International

I have known Chuck Rudolph for 45 years. In all that time I have never seen a major crack in his spiritual life. He has worked with me in two churches as well as Youth for Christ. I can totally recommend this book in its honesty and the way it has affected those who attended Chuck over his 4 year battle with Melanoma.

Pastor Gary S. Bawden

You will be truly blessed as you read about Chuck's journey fighting cancer. His insights should both encourage you and help you on your own journey which you may be traveling. To God be the Glory!"

Pastor Jericho J Bertholet

Pack full of genuine, heartfelt and gut-wrenching stories of the journey through cancer, this book is a diamond; a true gemstone. As you read you will be drawn into Chuck's journey, I couldn't put it down, it was that engaging. Wherever your journey in life has you, you will find comfort, peace, hope and encouragement. Chuck wrestles with real questions, real dilemmas and real decisions that he and his family faced as they looked over the cliff of death several times. Yet, what you will find is hope and faith beaming as bright as the noonday sun. Always careful to be honest and honoring, this volume acknowledges God's providential care in the middle of very difficult circumstances and situations. Read this book and buy several for friends, it's that good!

John Zivojinovic, Ph.D., President, Legacy University

A JOURNEY THROUGH CANCER

With Faith and Hope

By
Chuck Rudolph

With Evelyn Rudolph and Meloni S. Rudolph

WESTBOW®
PRESS
A DIVISION OF THOMAS NELSON
& ZONDERVAN

Scriptures taken from the Holy Bible, New International Version®, NIV®.
Copyright © 1973, 1978, 1984, 2011 by Biblica, Inc.™ Used by permission of
Zondervan. All rights reserved worldwide. www.zondervan.com The "NIV"
and "New International Version" are trademarks registered in the United
States Patent and Trademark Office by Biblica, Inc.™ All rights reserved.

This book is a work of non-fiction. Unless otherwise noted, the author
and the publisher make no explicit guarantees as to the accuracy of
the information contained in this book and in some cases, names of
people and places have been altered to protect their privacy.

WestBow Press books may be ordered through booksellers or by contacting:

WestBow Press
A Division of Thomas Nelson & Zondervan
1663 Liberty Drive
Bloomington, IN 47403
www.westbowpress.com
1 (866) 928-1240

Because of the dynamic nature of the Internet, any web addresses or
links contained in this book may have changed since publication and
may no longer be valid. The views expressed in this work are solely those
of the author and do not necessarily reflect the views of the publisher,
and the publisher hereby disclaims any responsibility for them.

Any people depicted in stock imagery provided by Thinkstock are
models, and such images are being used for illustrative purposes only.
Certain stock imagery © Thinkstock.

ISBN: 978-1-4908-7460-9 (sc)
ISBN: 978-1-4908-7459-3 (hc)
ISBN: 978-1-4908-7458-6 (e)

Library of Congress Control Number: 2015904720

Print information available on the last page.

WestBow Press rev. date: 04/07/2015

Contents

Foreward

It is my distinct pleasure and privilege to write the foreward to this book by my patient Mr. Chuck Rudolph. The manuscript is a firsthand accounting of a patient's and his family's physical, emotional and spiritual journey through the diagnosis and multiple therapies for malignant melanoma. The story of the Rudolph's life with cancer is a story of empowerment, humanity, family and faith. In my profession, we tend to so focus on the active medical issues at hand that we frequently only catch a glimpse of the life stories of our patients whom we struggle to save. I remember when I first read this book, I was overwhelmed by the emotional and spiritual depth of events that I myself was involved in, and was only minimally aware. Through every PET scan, every treatment, every procedure, and every bad report, the Rudolph's found strength to keep forging ahead. The day-by-day accounting and the prayer list updates say it all. From the depths of despair to the heights of elation, the Rudolph's journey through cancer is a testament to the human spirit. A beautiful story about an impossible, life changing event. I am honored to have been the Rudolph's doctor, and am a better person for having read their story.

Dr. Svetomir Markovic, Oncologist, Mayo Clinic (Rochester, MN)

This book is dedicated to my grandchildren: **Luke, Ema, Tessa, Ellie,** and any others who may come along.

You are the apples of my eye; and add brightness to my day each time I think of you.

There are so many people to thank that I am sure I will miss some if not many who are deserving of so much gratitude from us.

Evelyn, who for many years has been in my eyes the perfect example of the Godly woman in Proverbs 31. And who has stood with me on this long and painful (for both of us) journey. I believe you are the most courageous woman I have known.

Our children, Meloni, Aaron, and Amy: who have had to watch their father go through this trial. And wonder if we have had our last breakfasts together.

Aaron's wife Astrida, and Amy's husband Dan.

Bill and Kathy (my sister) and Jim and Sylvia (Evelyn's sister), who, living so close have carried such a load for us. From mowing to snow plowing to hauling us back and forth to Mayo Clinic to hundreds of other things you have done; we could not have gotten through this without your help.

Our Sunday School class: who let me teach whenever I was able, even though sometimes I was so weak I had to sit rather than stand. You know I love to teach, and getting ready for Sunday was very therapeutic for me.

Our niece, Norma: who being a Doctor of Nursing, helped in so many ways.

The 2nd Half class at Grace Chapel who continued so close to us, even after we moved to Minnesota; I look forward to sharing the stories in heaven of what all your cards, letters and prayers meant to us.

So many of our friends and siblings who helped with meals or took us back and forth to Rochester for the radiation cycles or other things: The physical rest I received while riding rather than driving was more important than we will ever know.

Dr. Markovic, our oncologist, who always had a next step and was so positive in outlook: We have grown to appreciate him so. He also made suggestions on this book, especially the medical language.

Dr. Ben Kipp, our nephew, who was always available to help me understand what was happening in a more complete way and from a different perspective.

Bob (Evelyn's brother) and Linda: for letting us stay in your home with you so often.

All the nurses and other medical personnel (at Rochester, Fairmont, and Eau Claire): who always took such good care of me, as your patient, and of all who came to visit me.

All who prayed regularly for us (at least 1000 that we know of): I wish I could go around and thank each of you personally. But that will have to wait until we reach Eternity.

To all of these, and others I am sure to have missed: Only Eternity will show how much you have meant to us, and to others who have been brought into your path.

An Introduction

As the cancer was attacking my body, and we did not know what would be the outcome, my grandchildren (Luke, Ema, and Tessa; Ellie has come along since my healing) were too young to understand the concern their parents had for me.

So I wanted to write this for my children, to help them retell these things to my grandchildren; and for others in the family and beyond to know that what I have experienced is nothing if not a miracle by the hand of God in my life.

In Section 1, I will relate an overview of our journey. My wife Evelyn relates her remembrances of the culminating stay in Methodist Hospital. And I include updates to our prayer partners written by our daughter Meloni during that same stay.

In Section 2, I relate insights which I believe God gave me during the journey.

In Section 3, I am enclosing a number of the email updates we wrote at different steps in this journey. I hope these will also help you to see that you or your loved one is not alone in the enduring of a terrible disease or tragedy.

Section 1

Our Journey – An overview

This has always been OUR journey. It could never be described as my journey, because especially Evelyn (my wife of 46+ years) and our children along with so very many of our relatives and friends have gone through this with us in one way or another. So, to call it mine would not only be very incomplete, it would also be an untruth.

I have learned much over this journey of life that has taken this "detour" from what we had planned and thought our path would be. And I am hopeful that each of those referred to above have also learned much. I would be very honored if any of them could say that I have in some way impacted their lives for the Lord and for good. I can honestly say I have tried to honor God through this time, but I am sure whatever I have done has only been done with His strength.

Our journey with cancer started in early 2008. I had a mole on the outside of my left leg that had grown over a several month period. I had a regular checkup with my doctor and asked her to look at it. She did, and did not think it anything to be concerned about since it did not appear to be cancerous. However, since it did occasionally catch on the seam of my trousers when I would turn a certain way, I asked her to take it off. She removed it that day in her office, and sent it in (to wherever they send such things).

Chuck Rudolph

About two weeks later, she called me at my office one morning and said, "We need to talk...".

This was the beginning of a journey that would take me through 8 cancer-related surgeries, chemotherapy, 2 rounds of radiation, and 3 very new cancer drugs.

After two surgeries at the University of Colorado hospital, I was told they had nothing more for me. Since they did not refer me to anywhere else, and since they had not suggested we try chemotherapy or radiation, we decided that this may not be the time to lie down and die without a fight.

That very afternoon I called the National Cancer Institute and was not able to get in there. I called M.D. Anderson in Houston because I was told they have a great Melanoma cancer program. I could get in there, but not for several months; and since we did not think I had several months, we kept trying.

We had both grown up in Southern Minnesota, in the backyard of Mayo Clinic in Rochester. I had always thought it to be the "Mountaintop of Medicine"; but, to my chagrin, I had never thought of it in terms of specialty medicine. When we inquired of one of our nephews, who happens to work at Mayo in cancer research, about a program for melanoma, we found out they did indeed have such a program.

I am convinced God led us to Mayo. Certainly, He could have healed me without the help of any medicine, but for reasons known only to Himself, He chose in this case to use several forms of medicine at Mayo.

4

I would liken this to looking at Scripture and seeing how Jesus healed people differently. In some cases He would touch people and they would be healed, in other places He would simply speak and the malady would be gone. Sometimes, He would forgive sins and physical healing was the result. And in Acts we are told of folks being healed simply by having Peter's shadow go over them.

When we were able to get into Mayo Clinic on very short notice (less than two weeks), we moved most of our belongings to Minnesota quickly. Shortly prior to this, my mother had moved into an assisted living establishment, and her house was empty. My brothers and sister were very generous to let us stay in the house that I had grown up in.

Over the 5 years since we have moved back to Minnesota, we have made approximately 125 trips to Rochester. It is about two hours and 15 minutes each way, so it has been many, many hours on the road. I can also tell you where the biggest bumps are (or have been, as they have repaired some of the worst ones).

Shortly after moving to Minnesota, I was hospitalized because of the pain the tumors at the top of my left leg were giving me. During this time in the hospital, we started the chemotherapy and also the first round of radiation.

The chemotherapy, as it does to many who have it, made me very sick. The treatments continued after I left the hospital, and I became so ill and vomited so often and so hard that I tore muscles in my abdomen. This led to having to have hernia surgery, with another hospitalization.

The radiation treatments also continued after leaving the hospital. We had to make the trip each day for several weeks. These treatments also made me so exhausted; I would sleep nearly all of the time (except during the treatments and when I was being sick).

After we realized the chemotherapy was not working, because the tumors were continuing to grow, we discontinued the treatments. However, the radiation seemed to have some good success at the time.

After a few weeks, the cancer returned and again became very painful. On meeting with the pain doctors at Mayo, it was determined that I could receive what is commonly called a "pain pump". This is a piece of equipment that is placed under the skin in the abdominal region with a tube going around under the rib cage to the base of the spine. There it drips on the nerves that come from the area of pain. It is about the size of a hockey puck, and includes a reservoir that holds enough medication for several months (depending on dosage).

This was installed surgically, and immediately helped control the pain and discomfort in the area of the tumors. But it was still another hospitalization.

After having gone through the round of chemotherapy that did not work, and the round of radiation where they gave me as much radiation as I could have handled; as well as two new drugs (Yervoy and Zelboraf), and several more surgeries which took about two years; I had another major surgery in January of 2012.

In this surgery the team removed several tumors and nearly all of the lymph nodes at the top of my left leg, and cut away the dead skin that had been burned to leather by the radiation. Then, to cover the area where the skin had been, they cut out a piece of skin and muscle from my abdomen that looked somewhat like a Ping-Pong paddle and, while leaving the very end of the handle of the "paddle" still attached in its original position flapped this over to cover the area that had been exposed.

I can tell you for sure that it is difficult to make a stomach muscle act like a leg muscle!

They also took out all the cancer they could find; and, once again, we hoped they had gotten it all.

About two months after this surgery, we took another PET scan and found out that the cancer had returned again. There were three new tumors, of which only one could be radiated. We decided to go ahead and radiate the one, and planned to deal with the other two by freezing them later.

The radiation took two weeks, and ended on a Friday late in April. By the following Monday, I was in terrible pain, and began running a fever. Evelyn took me into the local emergency room and they promptly sent me by ambulance to Mayo in Rochester.

I remember arriving there, and after several hours in the emergency room was transferred to a room in Methodist Hospital (part of Mayo Clinic).

I do not remember much else at all for the next 3 weeks. They tell me I was delirious, and if anyone touched me even lightly I would cry out in pain. I had an infection that probably had begun in the material of the radiated tumor and spread through the whole body. While not giving up on me, the medical team had tried nearly everything they could think of to rally me. A number of them did not think I would leave the hospital alive.

My niece, who has a doctorate in nursing, had come over to stay with me for a time since Evelyn had to return home occasionally; she urged the medical team to try another direction in the treatment by treating my thyroid gland. They did this, and that is about when I began to come around.

On one of the first days I was conscious, I was asked if I knew what day of the month it was. Since I remembered I had gone in on April 30th, I replied that it must be about May 2nd or 3rd. Ha! It was May 20th!

As I began to get stronger, the doctors began to talk about my going to a convalescence facility to continue to heal; however, the last 2 or 3 days that I was in the hospital I gained a lot of strength and I was able to be discharged directly to home.

We did not know what the situation with the cancer at this time was.

Two weeks after going home, we returned for another PET scan to ascertain what the disposition of the cancer was.

We had the PET scan finished, and went up to our oncologist's office. We waited, and then heard steps coming quickly down the hall. As he opened the door, he was nearly shouting as he said, "It's not there; it's not there!" I was so astonished at what I thought he might be saying that I had to ask him, "What's not there?"

He said, "The cancer, I can't see any. I can't explain it, it's just not there."

It had disappeared! After all that had happened, it just disappeared!

I am absolutely convinced that God had reached down and had taken the cancer from my body. It was truly a miracle from Him. The idea that it can be explained away by the infection in no way takes anything away from the fact of it being God's doing.

At the time of this writing, it has been gone for 36 months, and I have had 12 PET scans to keep checking for it.

Now, Evelyn and I know that the Melanoma may return at some point. But for today, and each day the Lord gives us until that would happen, we just want to be grateful for however many days He gives us on this earth. We know we'll have an eternity together with the Lord; but for now we are happy to be here and content to praise Him from this perspective.

While I cannot say it was an easy journey in any way, I can say without a doubt that without the Lord it would have been impossible to get through.

If you or a loved one is going through cancer or deep water of any kind, I would urge you to turn to Him. Perhaps you could talk to a pastor who loves the Bible for help in this area.

But to get started, open a Bible to the gospel of John and read this. God will open Himself to you as you read.

Notes

Notes

Meloni's Updates

These updates to our prayer list were written by our daughter, Meloni, during the 5 ½ weeks of my hospitalization in Rochester, Minnesota. This was the final hospitalization before we found that the cancer had been taken away. During this time, many of the doctors and other staff thought I would not leave the hospital alive.

I am including these so that you can get a glimpse into some of the feelings that a family may go through. To that end, I hope they are helpful to you.

May 17, 2012

Hey Everyone,

I am writing today from the Mayo Clinic in Rochester, MN. Many of you may know that Dad has been here for 2 ½ weeks...

Many many things have been happening with Dad. He came in to the Fairmont ER with a fever and was transported to Mayo where he endured 5 days of excruciating pain that kept him from sleeping. The flurry of drugs they gave him to give him even a little relief have overwhelmed his kidneys which are now functioning at a very low level...10% was about what the doctors estimated his kidneys were functioning at. He also has had a fever on and off for this whole time which further affects his kidneys. The fever is caused by an infection which the doctors have not been able to definitively diagnose. Dad has been in and out of the Intensive Care Unit at least 3 times with his fever spiking each time and his ability to clearly communicate has been coming and going.

Late this afternoon, Dr. Markovic, Dad's oncologist sat with Mom and Aaron and I to talk about what he thought was going on. The three of us were optimistic after talking to him that Dad has a chance of bouncing back from this. Dr. Markovic says that while they cannot definitively diagnose the infection that Dad is fighting, he is fairly confident that the infection is in the radiated tumor, which in a backwards way can help the situation since an infected tumor cannot grow as fast.

One thing that Dr. Markovic said to us that I had not heard before from either Mom or Dad is that he has never done so many varying treatments on someone and have the cancer keep coming back like this. He light heartedly says that Dad is trying to make it a challenge for him...I have to say I really appreciated talking with the Doctor, he is very good at what he does.

Today has been a better day for Dad and for Mom and for my brother and sister and I than the last several have been. Today we had a dozen or so aunts, uncles and cousins stopping by to see Dad. Since Dad's room is very small, we filled up the waiting room and took shifts in the room.

Anyway, while we have more optimism today than yesterday, Dad (and Mom) definitely needs your prayers. We don't know how long he will need to be in the hospital with this current set of issues, so again, your thoughts and prayers would be appreciated. I will do my best to send updates from here in the days I will be in MN (until at least next Tuesday).

Thanks
Meloni (Chuck's daughter)

May 19, 2012

Hi Everyone,

I am writing again from Rochester with another update about my Dad. Not too much has changed since the last email, but he does seem to be slightly better than yesterday. The doctors are seeing an improvement in his kidney function, but there is still a long way to go for kidney function to be normal. He is in and out of awareness of who is in his room, where he is, what we are all doing, etc. But, as Mom joked, he is getting a little bossy and that is probably a good sign.

Yesterday, Mom and I were standing at the foot of the bed and he was instructing us to lift and move the bed up against the wall, but that we needed to move the golf clubs and bats and balls first. I said "I don't have my golf clubs with me today Dad..." and he said in a disappointed tone "yeah, I don't either...." We think that his confusion is likely because of all of the pain medication they needed to "throw at him" (according to the oncologist) to get his initial pain to go away in the first week he was here.

So, as far as family being around, Aaron is flying back to Philadelphia tomorrow and I will be heading back to Colorado on Tuesday unless anything changes between now and then. It doesn't sound like they will let him out of the Mayo Clinic anytime very soon. There are still a lot of tubes in him despite the fact that they removed a temporary medication/feeding tube yesterday, which was good news.

I am not sure what else to say about it right now. Mom and Dad are both still in need of your prayers. Specifically, Mom could use prayers for strength.... and Dad can use prayers for the swift recovery of his kidneys and that the pain would go away and stay away, and that he will bounce back yet again from this latest scary episode. His doctors seem amazed at how many times he has bounced back so we are hoping for another one....

Anyway, thanks again for your thoughts and prayers.

Meloni

Update on Chuck, May 22

Hey everyone,

Yesterday we got the results from an MRI on Dad's brain. The results did NOT show any cancer in his brain, which is great news. We did not get any indication though on why his mental state continues to be altered. The doctors say that it really could be any number of things right now, but certainly we wish that Dad would be able to communicate more clearly and be his old self.

Today is Day 22 of him having been in the hospital for this episode. I am not sure what to say about it really. Any improvements he has made have been in very small increments and that is obviously a bit difficult for us to see. We are thankful though that he is improving, however slightly. We all wish we could give him even a little relief from the pain, or some quality rest. At least for me, and I think I speak for all of my family; it is hard to feel so helpless.

Anyway, that is the latest. I will be traveling back to Colorado tonight and will be making travel plans to come back to MN soon.

Thanks again for your thoughts and prayers.

Meloni

p.s. I am starting to put your responses to these emails into a scrapbook, so please keep the thoughts coming and I will make sure Dad and Mom get them, so they can keep looking at it when they need the encouragement.

June 2, 2012

I am happy to send an overdue update to let you all know that Dad is bouncing back in a way we were all hoping and waiting for. He is talking and eating and making jokes and even walking for a short spell here or there. Yesterday I had the chance to talk to him on the phone for a few minutes (for the first time in 32 days!) and he sounded like his old self. It was so good to hear!

The next step is for him to be released from the Mayo Clinic hopefully on Monday or Tuesday of next week to be moved to the Fairmont Hospital for a period of physical rehabilitation. He is not quite to the point of being able to go straight home, but he is doing much better! One of the doctors, when we all had a meeting on Wednesday used the words "dramatic improvement" about Dad's progress in the last few days.

So, again, I know this update is overdue...but it's good news. We are thankful for Dad's turnaround and are confident he'll be back doing things that relax him (like yard work and using various power tools) very soon.

Thanks for all your thoughts and prayers! We have all felt them and appreciate them.

Meloni

Update on Chuck June 8, 2012

Hello Everyone!

I am happy to report that at long last Dad is out of the Mayo Clinic as of Wednesday. I am even happier to report that he is HOME (as opposed to the Fairmont Hospital first, and then home.)

Mom says he is sleeping a lot and doesn't have much of an appetite, but he is doing well enough to be home, and right now, that is miraculous. He is watching TV tonight which he hasn't really been able to do for a while either, so we are hoping that a restful convalescence at home will bring him back to 100%. In the meantime, he is not in any severe pain other than minor aches from sleeping and being in bed a lot.

Thanks so much to each of you for your thoughts and prayers.

Meloni

Notes

Evelyn's remembering the 5 ½ weeks
in Rochester at the climax of our journey

Monday, April 30th, 2012

Chuck was having severe pain and had a fever of 103+, so we went to the ER in Fairmont, MN. They knew him by first name there, as he had frequented the ER often. We were there a few hours and they decided to send him by ambulance to Rochester Mayo Clinic. I went home to pack some things and stayed there for the night, made sure everything was OK to leave for a few days.

They checked him into the ER at ST Mary's Hospital and then moved him over to the Methodist Hospital in Rochester to the 4th floor. That was good, because we were most familiar with that area.

The morning came, after what seemed to be a restless night. Chuck called me and asked me to bring a few things. He sounded good at that point. Not long after that I was on my way to Mayo and got there in about 2 hours. When I got to Chuck's room there were about a dozen people (Doctors and nurses). Chuck was moaning, groaning and yelling in pain. He wasn't able to sleep for 4 days and nights, because they were not able to get the pain under control. Several different teams of professionals came in at various times and would ask him what his pain level was. It was usually a 9. They would come in so often, he said, "I just told you, it's a nine." As I said before, he didn't sleep for 4 days and nights. I just couldn't believe they could not get rid of the pain. He wouldn't eat anything of course.

When Chuck was in ICU, I would stay at the hospital overnight; otherwise I would stay at the home of my brother and his wife, Bob and Linda. It was so wonderful of them to let me stay there.

The 5th day, Saturday, May 5th I came to his room in the morning and he was not there and I was a little afraid he may have died. They had moved him to ICU on 10th floor, because his temperature had spiked, but after 36 hours his fever went down, not to what it should be, but down. So they moved him down to 4th floor again in a different room.

His pain was being controlled by meds now, and he must have been catching up on sleep, because it was difficult to wake him up. I would say "Chuck" and he would wake up just for a few seconds and close his eyes with no emotion in them. I would try to feed him and he would just take one bite and say "no more" and push my hand away. If I tried to feed him anymore, he would get upset.

He would not watch TV (not even his favorites). He was that way for several days.

I went home to East Chain, off and on, to work at my job at Martin County Youth for Christ. I would also catch up on washing clothes, paying bills etc. Friends and family were doing the mowing, watering, picking up the mail, etc. I would then come back to Rochester and stay with Bob and Linda. That was such a blessing to come to their place at the end of the day, and talk to them about the day, relax and have a good night's sleep.

Most of the time in the mornings, Bob would be up when I got up; and he would make us toast and oatmeal for breakfast. I was so thankful for such a good start for my day.

I came in on the 8th day and once again they had taken Chuck to the ICU with a high fever. They kept him there for about 36 hours, and brought him down to the 4th floor again; same nurses, different room.

On May 14th (over two weeks of hospitalization) the Doctors said they needed to talk with the ones of us who were there. Amy, Dan, Ema, Kathy, Bill, and I met with about a dozen medical professionals. It was a very daunting situation. We walked into a room where 12 professionals were lining the walls and they asked us to sit down. I knew at that point it wasn't good.

They said that Chuck's kidneys were shutting down, and that we might have to decide what to do. They said we may have to put him on dialysis and a feeding tube, because he wasn't eating enough. The staff also decided not to move him to the ICU anymore, because moving him was not helping his situation, and bringing him back to a different room was adding to confusing him. So they scheduled staff in his room around the clock.

During the 4th week I needed to go home, work, and catch up on things again, and my niece, Norma, wanted to stay with Chuck while I was gone. Since she is a Doctor of Nursing at Mankato State University, I signed a permission slip so she could look at what Chuck had been through, and what was going on, so if she had any ideas that might be helpful.

While she was there, she was pleased with what the professional staff had been doing for Chuck, but she did suggest that they give him Thyroid medicine. They started the Thyroid medicine; Chuck started to come around a little more. I started seeing a glimmer of hope.

The days plugged along and Chuck got a little better each day, eating a little more, watching TV a little and still sleeping much of the time. His kidneys had gotten worse, and we almost had to make a decision about dialysis, when the numbers started to get better.

During the 5th week of the stay he was getting close to the limit the Insurance would allow him to stay, so the social workers started looking for nursing homes where Chuck could go. He wasn't good enough to go home; he needed rehab, he was very weak. So they did that while we tried to get some strength built up.

Up until a few days before he was scheduled to leave the hospital, we thought he would go to a nursing home, but he improved a lot and so they let me take him straight home. What wonderful news that was.

On June 6th Bill and Kathy (Chuck's sister and brother-in-law) brought their van over to Mayo and helped me get Chuck home. He was so glad to get home after the 5 ½ weeks in the hospital.

He felt insecure the first week or two when I left him at home to go to work. After a few weeks, he was still a little weak, but started to gain strength faster and was OK with me going to work.

Two weeks later, we went over to Mayo to have a PET scan which would tell us the status of the cancer. We went through the normal schedule of the day; blood work, PET scan, lunch, pain clinic, and then to the Oncology clinic to see Dr. Markovic.

We waited just a few minutes and then Dr. Markovic came bounding in, all excited and exclaimed, "It's not there", "It's not there." We looked at him and each other in amazement. We weren't expecting that answer, so it was a complete surprise.

Chuck Rudolph

Dr. Markovic was so excited, because he doesn't usually have good news like that to tell people with Melanoma. I remember my stomach not having that achy feeling which I so often had when Chuck was going through the cancer. I just thought, WOW!!

God, Dr. Markovic and the wonderful team of physicians and nurses pulled Chuck through. We are so grateful.

Notes

Notes

Section 2

Why me?

Here is one of the most used questions in all of human experience. It comes in many forms, and we see it in the youngest of children (right after they learn the word "no!").

Sometimes, it would be "Why do I have to do this?"; or "Why can't my brother (or sister) do it instead of me?"; or "Do I have to be the one?"

Certainly it could be understood if it is uttered when someone gets cancer or another malady. But it can be a very dangerous question if someone dwells on it for a long period of time.

If one spends much time on this question, it begins a downward spiral to bitterness and self-pity; and you become a person who no one wants to be around; and who then feels even sorrier for himself or herself.

The question can also be turned around and be used when something very good has happened to you.

My father died a number of years ago now, and I remember him telling me some of the stories of World War II when he was fighting in Europe. They were going across France under General Patton, and fighting many battles.

Dad was decorated several times, and according to his buddies that he stayed in touch with after the war should have been decorated many times. After his buddies told me this, I asked him about it and he replied "I was just doing my job...". He may not have received all the medals he should have had, but he was certainly more of a hero in my eyes because of his humility and care for his men (who all thought he never got the credit he deserved).

Dad was a supply sergeant, and to men fighting on the ground in the cold of winter in Northern France, the man who was responsible for them getting warm clothing and blankets along with good, warm footgear. No army has ever been able to win a war without good supplies. And Dad apparently went out of his way to be sure his guys had the best equipment available, and the men in his battalion never forgot him.

One of his duties was to go around to each platoon each afternoon when they were setting up camp for the night, and get the list of each one who had been killed or wounded that day and prepare a report to go up the line to headquarters.

On one particular afternoon that he told me about, he made his rounds, and found that they had lost more men than usual that day, including two of his good friends. When he got back to the supply tent, he was so taken by this that he got down on his knees by the bumper of his Jeep and cried out to God, "Why me? ...why am I still living today and they are not?"

But no matter in what context or setting the question is asked, there really is only one answer that is satisfactory. Only one response that will keep a person from getting on that downward spiral to internal agony and bitterness:

That answer is found in the Bible. The book of John, chapter 9. For years before cancer struck my body, I had loved this story that John relates. Many of us know it as the story of the man born blind. I had loved this story for several reasons during this time, but after cancer came I saw it for another reason that helped get me through this great question of "Why me?"

Yes, I did ask this question; but because of this passage in the Bible, I did not have to dwell on it long.

In verse 2, the disciples ask the question of Jesus; "Who sinned, this man or his parents that he was born blind?" or "Why him?"

They ask it in the third person, but if the man himself had been asking, it would have come out "Why me?" or "Why did I have to be born blind?" or "Why not that man over there?"

Jesus answers, "...no one sinned. This happened so that God could be glorified".

You see, Jesus knew before time began that He would be walking down this road on that very Sabbath day, and at that very hour when the man would be sitting at this exact spot and Jesus and the disciples would stop and the question would be asked.

God wants to be glorified in our lives. And whatever He allows to happen to us, He wants us to respond in a way that will bring glory to Him in front of other people.

Did I ever grow to enjoy having cancer? No, I did not; but when I came face to face with the reality of this fact, then I was able to go ahead and give the glory and credit to God for what He was doing in my life.

And no matter what the situation or setting we find ourselves in when we ask the question; the only answer is to recognize that God wants to be glorified through it.

Notes

Notes

Not Alone

One of the very first things Evelyn and I did after we learned that I had cancer was to commit that we would not go through it alone. To this end, we began a list of email addresses of folks we would keep updated on my condition, and ask them to pray regularly for us.

We chose not to go with a Caring Bridge site because a few of the folks on the list were not believers, and we did not think they would go to a Caring Bridge site regularly; and we wanted to share where we were spiritually in the journey as a regular part of our updates. In many ways, a Caring Bridge site would have been easier for us, but we were trying to keep in mind what we felt was God's purpose for us to go through this in the first place – that of bringing some kind of Glory to Him.

So whenever we would know anything new, or be anticipating something coming up in the schedule, we would send out an email. We always thanked them for their prayers on our behalf, and would ask them to pray specifically for us in whatever we were going through.

This list grew over time to about 200 email addresses, and a number of folks on the list would forward them on to others (families, friends, or even whole churches). We know that there were over 1,000 people receiving the email updates and praying for us on a somewhat regular basis.

To each email update we would send out, we would receive a bunch of responses (up to 50). These responses were always a great encouragement to us. Many of them brought tears to our eyes as people would tell how they had been encouraged by our message at a time when God was working in their lives as well.

Our greatest encouragements came when we would receive a reply from one who we were not sure they knew the Lord. Several of these have developed over the months into pretty good pray-ers! And conversations I have had with them lead me to believe they now know the Lord, and when the Lord has called us both home, the two of us can have some long conversations there in Heaven.

As I look back over this journey (and <u>journey</u> is the right word for it!), I cannot fathom having had to go through it alone. All of these folks held us up in so many ways, both spiritual and physical, that I just know that we would not have gotten through it all if we had tried to do it alone.

On nights when the pain from the tumors would be so great that all I could do was to lay on the bed in a fetal position and cry out to God to take me home; and all Evelyn could do was to hold me; I had this very real (to me at the time) picture in my mind of hundreds of people holding us above their heads with outstretched arms toward the Father's throne. I know that I will carry this picture in my head through the grave and into Eternity with the Lord Himself.

Another reason I am very glad we went the way we did was that we stayed away from church prayer chains (at least for the most part). Over the nearly 40 years I have spent in ministry, I have seen some very good ones, and I have also seen some very bad ones. The bad ones either go the direction of the old game of Telephone, where one person calls another, that person is to pray and then call another, etc. By the time it gets through the list, the prayer request can go from praying for minor surgery to praying for the family of the one lost in surgery!

Another negative prayer chain would be where people really only use it as a source of gossip. I know of churches where people do not call in for prayer, because they do not want to be the subject of gossip.

Hebrews 10:22-25 speaks of drawing together to encourage and lift up one another. Certainly the traditional view of this is to meet together on Sundays; but it would also include coming together to pray for and hold up people to the Lord. When used in a right way, and with the right motives, this should also be a way of encouraging everyone involved in the process; including both the one(s) prayed for as well as the ones praying.

I remember Chuck Swindoll using an illustration of pioneers settling the land across America. They would file their homestead claim (or whatever papers were required in their region), and then go and build a house or a sod hut on the highest hill they could find closest to the middle of their property. You see, they didn't think they needed anyone around them; they could make it on their own; by their own stubborn will. And many pictures can now be found in old albums or in museums of these folks. You have probably seen some yourself; they are the ones where the people have the sunken, hollowed out eyes, and are never smiling.

Thankfully, many of these found their own answers to the loneliness their isolation had caused themselves and their families. They moved down to one of the corners of their farm, across the road from 2 or 3 of their neighbors. There they could fellowship with others, they could help and be helped when that was needed, and their children had others to play with. They could have a life that had satisfaction for a day's work done well, and Sunday afternoon picnics.

In many instances, these 3 or 4 family enclaves became named settlements or villages. These also many times saw the starting of small churches.

Most of these enclaves are gone now, pushed aside to make room for bigger and still bigger machinery to farm larger and larger farms, but when we are facing a huge physical malady like cancer (or anything, for that matter) we do ourselves well not to forget the lesson of those pioneers living alone.

I am sure that some will say that they are (as the old song says) <u>Never Alone</u>. And, in the sense of that song, we are not alone because we have Christ with us. His Holy Spirit indwells us. But God did not make us to go through things alone as humans. He made us with an innate need to be together; to be encouraged and helped; and also to encourage and help those around us.

I can honestly tell you that when we have been in the waiting rooms over at Mayo Clinic, I can look around and show you people who are on both ends of this spectrum: some have family and friends around them, and can even smile occasionally in the face of news that is not-so-good. Others are all alone and even have begun to show the sunken eyes and permanent look of unhappiness that those pioneers did when living alone.

Evelyn and I have been privileged to live in Colorado for a number of years. When we lived there, we would often drive into the mountains. Doing this, one becomes very familiar with tunnels.

In a real way, this journey with cancer has been like going through a very long tunnel. Way ahead, one can see the light of the Lord at the end of the tunnel, and this is where we keep looking, but the tunnel itself is very dark as one gets into it.

But each prayer that is sent up to carry us through also is like a candle to show us the rocks in the road to avoid as we go to the end, which seems so far away.

If you are going through a disease like this, please do not try to go through it alone. Rather, find some folks (your family, or close friends, or your pastor) to come alongside you. I can assure you that the journey ahead of you will be ever so much easier for you.

Or, if you know someone who is beginning a journey like this, come alongside him or her and let them know you will walk the road ahead with them. Maybe you cannot be with them daily, or even weekly, but letting them know you care could mean everything to them.

There is an old saying: A burden shared is half a burden, and a joy shared is double joy. That will be the way with you at every turn in your journey ahead.

Notes

Notes

Loneliness

What I'd like to talk about now, for just a little bit, may come off sounding like I am complaining; and I do not want to sound that way; but if I don't talk about it, you may never realize just how easy it can be to help someone with a malady which keeps them inside.

What I want to talk about is loneliness.

In the 1700's, 1800's, and early 1900's when a missionary would leave his or her shore, he or she would say good-bye knowing not only that perhaps they would never see their family and friends again, but also that they would be very alone where they were going. Often it would take a letter many months to get from them to home or home to them.

These missionaries' braved new shores and untold dangers for the cause of Christ. I am sure there was a great deal of loneliness involved with these great men and women. Only eternity will tell the great difference made in the lives of millions of nationals by these our forerunners.

But, and here is the difference, they were called and, after counting the costs, chose to go.

When a person is made a shut-in because of a disease or accident, he has not had a chance to count the cost of being alone or to prepare himself for this kind of loneliness.

Even with so many people praying for us, and the often received emails, there were days when I would need to be left alone for several hours at a time. During these times even I would feel lonely; sometimes desperately lonely. I so wanted someone to stop by and talk, or just call and say "hi".

And even with our friends and relatives only a block away, I would be lonely.

So, I cannot help but think of others who are truly alone in our community or in your community who are probably feeling even lonelier than I ever could have been.

I believe there are 2 primary vehicles of caring for the person who is shut in, either temporarily or for an extended time. These are a person's family and their church.

I know that if we are a Believer in Christ, we are never really alone; He is always with us. But I also know that as Believers, we are part of a body much greater than the physical body I reside in. And when any part of that body is hurting, other parts of that body must help it through the pain and help it to heal.

If anyone in your family or church is shut in (especially with a painful malady), please set up a rotation so someone calls them or stops in to see them every day. Only Eternity will show you how great a ministry you will have had.

If you are a shut-in, please reach out to someone and let them help you. The Bible gives instructions for us to care for one another when one has a need like this.

If you refuse to let someone help you, you not only lose the blessing of their help; but you also prevent them receiving a blessing for helping you.

The whole idea of helping one another is one of the great needs we all have. Belonging to a church is the best way I know to be a part of such a great blessing for everyone.

If you are not a part of a local church; please, for your own sake, find a Bible believing and Bible teaching church and become a part of it. It may be the best step you could ever take!

Notes

Notes

Chuck & Evelyn, with their children (& spouses), and all their grandchildren.

Chuck and Evelyn near where they lived in Colorado

Chuck and Evelyn near their 45th Anniversary.

Giants

We all know the story of David and the giant, Goliath. It is one of the best loved Bible stories for all ages.

The Israelite army was facing the Philistine army across a valley, and the armies were yelling across at their opponent trying to get an advantage. But one day, the yelling (on the Israelite side, anyway) stopped. This huge man, Goliath, came out and defied the Israelites, their king (Saul), and even God Himself.

He was over 9 feet tall!

After he had challenged the Israelites for many days, with the Israelites cowering away from him, the lad David came to visit his brothers, who were in the army. When David heard the insults being thrown by the giant, he wanted to fight him. He could not tolerate anyone defaming his God.

Prior to this, the Bible tells us that David had already fought a lion and a bear that had tried to steal his sheep. Both of these situations had served to bolster his faith in God.

Now he goes confidently to fight this battle. He is confident because God has helped him in the other battles.

Can you imagine how hopeless his situation looked to all the other soldiers, on both sides? Here is a young boy going up against this giant who is sure to kill this upstart youngster!

But David knew something no one else recognized; that God was on his side, and would make the little stone go right where it was supposed to, and that God would get the glory for this victory.

So he puts a stone into the sling, twirls it around and lets it go. It goes into the forehead of the giant and kills him! And God was praised for this and for the great victory over the Philistines that followed.

I believe we will all probably face several "giants" in our lives. Each one is meant to build our faith in God, and also to bring God the glory. These could come in the form of sickness, death of loved ones, financial problems, or any one of a hundred other happenings.

Let me give you a definition of a giant: A giant is anyone or anything that defies your faith in God. In other words, if anything you face calls into question either the power of God, or makes you think of giving up on God, that is a giant.

There have been a number of "giants" in my (our) life prior to the onset of the melanoma cancer. I will share just 2 of them.

I started to work for Youth for Christ in September of 1973. Through a specific set of circumstances, we actually started to work before all of our support had been raised. By Christmas of that year, we still did not have it all in; and we received just what did come in, which was enough to pay the rent and a little for groceries.

We needed and wanted to go back to our families' homes for the holidays, but did not know if we could; because we had only enough gas to get there, and the tires on our old Chevrolet Vega were bare.

We decided to trust God for all of this, and to go. We made it to my parents' house on the evening of December 23rd. The gas tank was nearly empty, and one of the tires was showing the wires under the rubber treads.

The next morning, Christmas Eve, at the breakfast table, Mom said, "I'm sorry, this envelope came for you yesterday, and I forgot to give it to you last evening." If asked, she would say she was too happy to see us, and to play with our 1 ½ year old daughter; but I believe God used even this to bolster our faith, because in the envelope was a check from one of the Sunday School classes at our church. It was for $78 dollars.

I immediately called every tire shop in town, and found a set of 4 tires for $76 dollars, and if I hurried in, they would install them by noon.

And at the price of gas back then, the other 2 dollars filled the tank on the Vega with more than enough to get us back to our home again!

God used this to show us that He can be trusted to supply all of our needs.

A few years later I was in Mexico City for a mission project. Since I had been there several times, and knew how bad the traffic was, I had my host take me to a hotel near the airport on the evening before my flight back to the states for a meeting the next afternoon.

My flight was scheduled for 6 AM, so I was up and ready to leave the hotel at 4 o'clock. I asked at the desk for a shuttle, and was told it would not run until 6:30. And the man at the desk said if I walked, and went out the gate, I would not be able to get back in until 6 o'clock.

I felt I had no choice; I needed to catch that particular flight to make the important meeting. So, knowing where the airport was and how to get there, (only about 6 blocks) I went through the gate and heard it slam behind me.

After about two blocks, I came on a big trench which I had not seen before. They were digging the subway route to the airport. In the dim light, I could see a narrow wooden makeshift bridge spanning the chasm. As I started across it, I realized there were a number of men on the other side who were squaring off to fight with each other.

I did not want to go across, but I knew I could not go back; and I did need to make that flight.

So I did what in my mind up to that time would have been unthinkable; I prayed for God to protect me, and began to walk forward.

I walked with my luggage through the crowd of men and not one of them challenged me; or even seemed to notice me! Somehow God had protected me and through it had taught me He can protect me in any situation.

Again my faith in Him was bolstered.

Chuck Rudolph

God has often shown me that He is able to provide for and protect me through any storm of our lives.

This journey with melanoma has, without a doubt, been the biggest goliath I have ever had to face. And I can say again that God is able to be trusted.

Friend, please put your trust in Him; first of all for your Salvation. He died on the cross of Calvary to pay for all you have ever done wrong, and He rose again to New Life so that you also can have life with Him now on this earth, and forever with Him in Heaven.

And once you have done this, then know that He is able to be trusted for every aspect of your life. He can provide for and protect you in whatever you are facing.

Notes

Notes

How will I provide for my family?

I come from good, solid, northern European stock. One of my great-grandfathers came from Germany in 1881, having stowed aboard a ship in a potato barrel. They were 3 days out to sea when he was discovered, and they took all the money he had for his passage; besides making him work the rest of the way across to America.

Once here, he became a farmer and by the time of his death owned 4 farms; all completely paid for. He had 6 children, 4 sons and 2 daughters. My father's birth mother died from complications of his birth, and he was adopted by one of these two aunts. At that time, adoption within the family was quite common, but you did what you had to do to protect the family, especially children.

While I was growing up, my father would, from time to time, tell us how grateful he was to have been adopted this way. And this aunt who had adopted him, along with her husband were always "Dad" and "Mother" to him. All of us called them Grandpa and Grandma Rudolph. Dad often made the point of these folks having chosen him to love.

To me, this has always been a great illustration of what it means to be adopted into the family of God when we place our trust in Him. There are very practical blessings that come to the one who has been adopted.

My parents went out of their way to protect and provide for us. It was a great example to learn by, and I have always tried to do the same for my children and grandchildren.

But, when the reality struck home that this cancer very well could cause me to no longer be able to provide for or protect my children; it threw me for a loop for a time.

Questions like "How will they get along without me?" and "Who will care for them?" went round and round in my head.

I did not want them to go through life without my counsel; although my children were all adults who were doing well at the time. And I truly believed that no child should grow up without grandparents to love and spoil them. (Of course, I am sure that my wanting to see and enjoy my grandchildren growing up had nothing at all to do with my feeling helpless!?!)

But, when I came on the verse where God keeps track of the sparrows and cares for them; and when I had to admit that I was not the only sparrow in the barnyard, then I could start to think more clearly on this subject.

And the only conclusion I could come to was that the Lord Jesus could take care of each of them better than I could ever think of doing.

And this fact includes Evelyn, my wife, as well as my children and my grandchildren.

So, I began to think of what I could do for each of them in the time I had left.

Certainly, I could keep in touch as much as possible. We talked on the phone and in person whenever possible. We also used the Skype program on the computer often.

But one thing that I began to do for them, actually helped me as much as it could ever help them. I began to write letters to each of them that, in essence, would be the last thing I would say to them on this side of Heaven.

Before each surgery that I would go through, I would write (or update) a letter to each of them. As I would finish each one, I could feel that I had constructed it to be what I wanted and needed to say to each one. Then I would give this packet of letters to a trusted friend with the instructions to deliver them only if I did not make it through the surgery. So far, none of them have been delivered, and only the last batch exists.

The ones to my grandchildren had an extra instruction and that is that they were to be delivered to each one on their 12th birthday. In this way, I felt they would be able to understand more, and also to be able to ask better questions of their parents and grandmother.

I hoped that what I said in each letter would be taken for what it was: the last words of a man who cared deeply for them; and even though gone now, still loved them and wanted to see them flourish on this earth, and then join me in heaven where we could enjoy each other for an eternity.

Doing this also helped me greatly. By crystalizing thought in this way, it showed me not only what was important to say when I thought I was dying; it also showed me what to say while I am still living.

Notes

Notes

The Eastern Gate

During the long sleepless nights of my journey, and especially when the pain was so great that I could not in my own strength bear it; I had a picture in my mind of going into Heaven and leaving this body with its pain behind.

In Philippians chapter one, when Paul speaks of being absent from the body, and present with the Lord; I take this to mean that the moment our body dies, we are immediately (or at least momentarily) with the Lord Jesus Himself. And during those hard times this is what kept my attention.

I am sure that some will argue with me theologically, but let me describe what I was seeing. In the song The Eastern Gate, by Isaiah G. Martin, there is a picture of the person being welcomed to Heaven just inside the Eastern Gate to that great and wonderful place. This was the setting for what I saw in my mind often during my three and a half years categorized as stage four Melanoma.

The gate would open, and I would be ushered in. The first person I would see would be my Lord, Jesus Christ. There was no mistaking Him, as He was the center of the group welcoming me home. I was always awestruck, even though nothing was ever said (I suppose because it just wasn't my time to go yet).

But I believe that the Lord allowed me this picture to let me know it will be a great time when I do arrive there.

And as I have studied that image in moments when the pain was not so great, I realize that I know many of the people gathered around the Lord to help welcome me there into the land where there is no more pain.

Just behind the Lord, and looking over His shoulders are my father and my older brother. On His right and left side were both of my grandmothers, who prayed often for me when I was growing up and as long as they were living.

While I do not know for sure how we each will appear to one another (or, what age we will see each other) each of the ones I could recognize in the picture were just as I like to remember them, and not as they looked when they were very old or close to death.

Others that I could see and identify were a great-grandmother; who did appear old, I suppose because she died when I was very young, and this would be the only way I could know her. She was joined by a good number of others who also seemed to be more ancient. I took these to be more of my ancestors, who we know from the stories handed down as well as research done, they also knew the Lord and because of this would also be there to greet me (and others close to me) when we each reach those golden streets in the picture.

Also there were friends from throughout my lifetime who had gone on ahead.

What a wonderful reunion each of us as Believers in Jesus Christ can look forward to.

In the picture that I saw, there were three more individuals that I have not yet met at all. They were young children, and I believe them to be those little ones who were miscarried by my daughter and daughter-in-law.

Those who believe life only starts at birth will be angry with me for including this part of the picture; but if, as the Bible teaches, that life begins at conception, then it follows that these precious ones would have been taken care of by God Himself and be there waiting for us. I so want to spend a great deal of time in Eternity getting to know each one of them.

Theologically, I do not know if this is exactly the way we will, as Believers in Jesus, be ushered into Heaven; and I would not try to argue the point, but I believe the Lord allowed me this image to get me through those days of terrible pain. But the other result of having this picture is that I long for it to happen in my life every day. I look forward to this with great anticipation.

But the important thing is that we have believed in Jesus Christ in this lifetime. In this way we can be assured of being there with Him as we die and exit this body.

Notes

Notes

Fully and Completely Healed

I can say with 100% certainty that if we are Believers in Christ, we will be fully and completely healed from any disease or malady we may be now or will suffer.

This will happen. The blood of Christ which was shed for us guarantees this. The only question left is when this will happen? Will it be in this body or the next?

During the longest and darkest months of our journey, I took heart often in the promise of Revelation 21:4. This is the promise of no more pain.

When I was in the greatest of pain, I needed the assurance this verse provides that when we are in Heaven and have our resurrection bodies we will have no more pain. This is truly good news!

Let me illustrate this great truth from another perspective: In John 9, the story of the man born blind, that I have referred to elsewhere is another look at the timing and direction God may take as He heals you and me.

In verse 6, Jesus spit on the ground, made mud with it, put it on his eyes, and told him to go and wash.

Now, why in the world do you suppose He did all this?

In other places, he:

- Simply touched people to heal them,
- Sometimes He spoke and they were healed,
- One time, a lady just touched his robe and she was healed,
- Over in Acts, if Peter's shadow went over a person, they were healed.

So why, would the Lord of the entire universe here; spit, make mud, put it on the eyes, and tell the man to go and wash?

While considering this, I was reminded about a couple of scenes from the films that have been made from C.S. Lewis' Tales of Narnia. In "The Lion, the Witch, and the Wardrobe" the youngest of the four children, Lucy, prays and Aslan comes to rescue them.

In either the 2nd or 3rd movie of the series (I don't remember which), we find them in need of rescue once more. Lucy prays again to be rescued as in the other time, and as she is asking for this, Aslan comes and rescues them from a completely different direction and in a different way.

After it is all over, and they have been rescued, Lucy is talking to Aslan and asks, "Why didn't you rescue us like you did before?"

Aslan answers very tenderly, "Lucy, you know I do not work in the same way more than once"...

(These quotes are my paraphrase)

On that Sabbath morning in John 9, It was the God of the Universe (Jesus) who knew from before time began that He would walk down that very lane on this exact Sabbath day, with His disciples, and they would come on this very man and the whole picture was put together to glorify Him!

So He (the Creator, the God of the Universe) spit, made mud, put it on the eyes and told him to go and wash.

If God had told me back in 2008 when I was diagnosed with cancer that He was going to heal me in this body, I would have probably shouted, "Why not right now?" or, "let's get it over with!" But He had other purposes in mind for this situation.

One result was to draw me closer to Himself. Another was to have nearly a thousand people become involved in praying for me, and then to let them see that He is still in the business of doing miracles. If He had chosen to not take the cancer from this body, (as it looked for many months may happen), then I hope I would have died with a smile on my face, knowing that I was finally not going to have any more pain.

He is still the Creator, He is still the God of the Universe, and He still wants to be glorified before others in you and me.

So, if you or someone close to you is suffering from a disease or from being hurt in an accident, He wants to be glorified in that situation.

You can certainly ask to be healed, and you can be completely assured that He will answer your prayer; but please just keep in mind that He wants to be glorified through you by having other people see you go through this with dignity and a great faith in Him. And it may bring the greatest glory to Him to heal you not in this body, but the next.

Below is an update we sent when we heard the good news that the cancer could not be seen.

July 5, 2012

We all can be praising the Lord today. I met with the oncologist yesterday, and the news was VERY GOOD. He said there is no evidence at all of cancer right now!!!!!!! He is somewhat guarded about what is happening as there is a lot of inflammation where the tumors were, and this inflammation may be masking some melanoma, but he doesn't necessarily think this is the case. He just says we have to wait for another PET scan in about 6 weeks, when the swelling has gone down. But this is such good news, he was almost jumping up and down when he told me there was no evidence of the cancer we have been battling for so long.

He stressed several times that we are not out of the woods yet, but he said we should be celebrating for the time being (so we are—we had an ice cream cone yesterday!)

As we talked about this journey we have been on, he said he had "thrown the whole arsenal at me". I pointed out that after everything had been done from a medical standpoint, apparently the Lord stepped in and healed me... a miracle. He would not argue with this.

The Lord does work in mysterious ways to bring Glory to Himself!

With all of our attention on the cancer for so long, we really have not been able to plan ahead very much, and I get excited about what may be ahead; but I thank the Lord for having taught me how to take each day as it comes... I know I needed that lesson along with probably lots of other things I needed to learn. My prayer is that I have been a good student on these lessons and have become more like the Savior through them.

We have all been in this together, and I trust it has been and will continue to be a good experience for you. I cannot thank you enough for all you have done for us and with us.

I will continue to keep you informed as we know more...

God bless,

Notes

Notes

One Day at a Time

I love the old hymns. The church we attended as I was growing up sang – a lot. I always enjoyed these because I could sing loudly and my voice would be lost in the great choir of the whole congregation. It was fun to be in church during the singing of those wonderful old songs.

Those songs have stayed with me. I don't remember all the words to all the songs, but I remember enough to be able to sing a verse or two of many of them.

Those songs really have meant a lot to me as I have been on this journey with the cancer. Particularly when the pain became greater, I would recite them to myself as a way to keep my attention off of myself and onto what God has done; both for me and all of us.

One of the ones that I would go over and over in my mind (and sometimes out loud) was:

> Turn your eyes upon Jesus,
> look full in His wonderful face,
> and the things of earth will grow strangely dim,
> in the light of His glory and grace.

These words, written many years ago by Helen H. Lemmel have brought to me much comfort in times of great trouble and pain. I am sure that it is just as precious to many others.

Another hymn that carried me through many long nights, especially when the pain was greatest, was one that is not quite so old. It was written by Bill and Gloria Gaither, and is titled "Because He Lives".

One particular line in that song kept me going during times when I could not sleep and would get very little rest. "... because He lives, I can face tomorrow..." This line kept (keeps) reminding me that it does not really matter if I wake up in this body or not; because, since He has come out of the grave and conquered death for me; I can be assured of waking up in His presence if I am no longer in this body racked with the ravages of cancer.

This entire song touches me deeply each time I hear it sung. I even have a wooden plague with the entire song lasered into it sitting in my office. It is included in the instructions I have left for my funeral (whenever that happens to occur). Can you tell I love this song?

Also during the many months when we did not know if I would live or die, the song "When the Roll is Called up Yonder, I'll Be There" was a staple for me.

On the nights when I would cry out to God to take me Home, this song would come to mind and be a great blessing to me. The pictures of Heaven it would bring to me were enough to take my mind off the discomfort of the body and point me to "... that bright and cloudless morning, when the dead in Christ shall rise..."

I hope you as a reader will indulge me a couple of comments on the music of our churches today.

First, let me say that I enjoy the new music too. Some of it does not have the catchy tunes that one leaves the church singing, but that is not so bad; I still enjoy singing them.

But my concern is not so much about the music itself, but about what it has taken away; and I am not thinking about the enjoyment of the old music, but the fact that when we look at a screen with only words and no notes and staffs; Who is teaching our young people and children to read music so they can enjoy it for all their lifetimes?

Many of our schools are going through tough times financially right now, and the arts (including music) are often one of the first things to be cut. The church can be a great asset to the culture of a community if it is teaching music to our next generations.

One last song that has meant so much to me is one that has been recorded by many folks on the country music charts: It is called "One Day at a Time".

The title of it says it so well; we must live just one day at a time. We cannot jump ahead to next week or next month, we have to live today first, right now.

For months in this journey with the cancer, in the morning I would think about how I would get through, not until tomorrow morning, but just until this evening; then in the evening, I would change my perspective and consider how I could make it through the night. In the morning, I would shift again to the day. This was the only way I could get myself through the long days and nights.

You see, "one day at a time" must be much more than a cliché, it must become our lifestyle. If we try to live next year right now, we lose sight of all the good things and great people God has placed around us to enjoy as we pass through this life.

There are many things around us, and happening to us, and certainly we are to plan for the future; but we must always remember that God is in control of our lives, and not we ourselves.

Notes

Notes

Great Faith

On June 30, 2003, as a nurse was helping my father get ready for bed that evening in the rest home; she saw him turn to her and say, "I won't be here in the morning".

She, knowing him quite well, said "Oh, Clem, I know you have had a hard day, but it will get better tomorrow..."

Dad said, "No, you don't understand. I won't be here; I will be with Jesus and with Melvin". (Melvin was my older brother who had died a year and a half before).

My father could sense that his body was shutting down, and that soon it would be his turn to go the way that all of us must go. He was a believer in Jesus, and he was looking forward to being with Him, his son, and all the other relatives that have gone on before.

Hebrews 11:1 says "Now faith is being sure of what we hope for and certain of what we do not see..."

The chapter then becomes the "Hall of Fame" of those who have faith; great faith, if you will, in God.

Dad did not live early enough in time to have been included in the list in Hebrews 11, but in my eyes he would still be included if the list continues in Heaven.

Looking down through the list there we can find some great names. And some of them have a lot written about them to commend them to this great listing. But some of them only get a little bit written there.

One of these is Joseph, in verse 22. "By faith Joseph, when his end was near, spoke about the Exodus of the Israelites from Egypt, and gave instructions about his bones." (NIV).

The only thing said about Joseph is his death bed statement.

Now, don't get me wrong, I believe a person can be on his death bed and become a believer and go to Heaven for all eternity. As a reference, I think of the man on the cross beside Jesus, who recognized the Lord for who He was; and Jesus responded with "... This day, you will be with me in Paradise..."

But this kind of conversion would not get you into a Hall of Fame of faith. If it did, it would be like an NFL team hiring a 65 year old quarterback who gets into only one game, throws one pass that is incomplete, and yet still makes the Hall of Fame in Canton, Ohio.

And it is not just the one statement recorded that gets Joseph there either.

The story of the life of Joseph is one of the best loved stories in the entire Bible.

He was not the oldest son of Jacob, but he was the oldest son of Jacob's favorite wife (Rachel). And as such he became the favorite son of his father. So much so that when the other brothers had to go out to work, Joseph stayed back with his father.

Joseph pushed the jealousy button in his brothers often, even telling them of dreams he had had where the brothers would bow down to him.

One day his father asked Joseph to take some food to the brothers. He did it, and when the brothers saw that they had him alone, they took him and threw him in a pit. Then they sold him to a caravan going to Egypt.

When he reached Egypt, he was sold into the house of Potiphar. His integrity was quickly recognized and he was put over the entire house, except, of course, for Potiphar's wife.

But, she wanted to sleep with him. He responded, "I cannot do this great sin against my master and my God..." Joseph must have learned a lot sitting by his father's feet back in Canaan.

Well, then she got disgusted with Joseph and had him put in prison. There, again his integrity was recognized by the warden and he was put over the other prisoners.

Later, two of the prisoners (who had both worked for Pharaoh) had dreams. They came and told Joseph the dreams. As he was interpreting the dreams, he said "the interpretations belong to God..."

His interpretations turned out perfectly. One of the men was restored to his position with the king, and the other lost his head. As the one was leaving the prison to return to Pharaoh, Joseph waved to him and reminded him, "Don't forget me!" And the butler promptly did forget him.

Two more years went by with Joseph in prison. He could have become bitter and angry, but he did not. Then, Pharaoh himself had a dream. He wanted someone to interpret it for him, but no one could. Pharaoh even threatened them all, but still nothing.

Then the butler remembered Joseph in prison. They called him, and gave him new clothes to see the king.

Along with the words "the interpretation belongs to God", Joseph interpreted the dream of the king and made the suggestion that the king appoint a wise man to oversee the grain and its use so that Egypt could get through not only the seven good years, but also the seven bad years.

Pharaoh agreed and appointed Joseph because he was the wisest man the king could find.

The seven good years came, and Joseph stored up all the grain he could. When the seven bad years came, he sold grain to the people to keep them alive in the famine.

But the famine was not just in Egypt, but also in Canaan. And Joseph's family needed grain to live, so the father sent Joseph's brothers to Egypt to buy grain.

When they came to Egypt, Joseph recognized them, but they did not know him.

It took two trips down, along with some manipulations, but then Joseph showed himself to them. He said, "You meant all this for evil, but God meant it for good…"

After this, the whole family came and lived in Egypt. They were taken care of by Joseph and Pharaoh. They were settled in the best part of Egypt, which was Goshen. Everything was provided for them... they had it made!

They lived there, and like all of mankind, got older. And when Joseph realized that he was going to die, he called the leaders together and told them that when they left Egypt, they were to take his bones along.

When he made this statement, it probably sounded very absurd to the others. After all, they had everything they needed in Egypt, why would they ever want to leave?

But Joseph knew God's plan. He knew that the land of Goshen was not the land that had been promised to his father and his grandfather and his great-grandfather Abraham. The land of Canaan was the Promised Land, and Joseph wanted to be always identified with the people and promises of God.

So he said "...take my bones..."

So, it wasn't just the death bed statement that got him into that great list of people of faith; it was a whole life lived by faith!

And it was a life that had very hard circumstances; at least as hard as any you or I could face, but...

Joseph knew the plan of God, and he trusted in the God of the plan.

My father knew the plan of God, and he trusted in the God of the plan.

God wants us to know His plan, and He wants us to trust in Him as the God of the plan.

You see, no matter how bad we may see our circumstances (cancer, broken bones, broken marriage, wayward children, etc.) He wants us to trust Him.

And the term "great faith" is somewhat of a misnomer. A better way to describe the faith of Joseph and the faith of my father would be "simple trust". And all God asks of us is to simply trust in His workings through our circumstances. He is in control, and He will do what is going to glorify Himself the most, and what is best for us (from His point of view).

Notes

Notes

Section 3

Some of the updates to our prayer list written by Evelyn and Myself

Update – June 24, 2011

Last evening, as we sat at the dinner table and looking out at the valley which has become so familiar and peaceful to me; it was truly an idyllic scene. Several species of birds were coming and going at the feeders, squirrels were playing in the trees (with one wanting to come and rob from the bird feeders), and a whitetail doe was grazing at the bottom of the hill. The creek beyond the fence is once again full due to nearly 5 inches of rain this last week, and the trees and brush are in lush bloom.

It was easy to get caught up in it all, and to just be together without having to say much at all to each other. Such is the peacefulness I dream of in Heaven. Until...

Entering from scene-left, we see a skunk!

Now, don't get me wrong, I know that God created this animal too; so I know he must have a purpose in the grand scheme of things. I just cannot think of any good reason at all from my vantage point! The skunk sauntered through the scene until he was behind our little shed and then disappeared into the bushes. I truly hope for good!

Life is a lot like that scene, I think. We can be going along on cruise control with everything happening our way, and then something very unfitting comes into the picture. Something that we can think of no good reason to happen to us, and that seems so unfair that it takes us off of the life track we were on so happily.

But just like that skunk, God doesn't put these things in our path to frustrate us, He puts them there for His reasons. We only need to accept that this is the case. His plan is ultimately to make us like Himself and to prepare us for that life with Him in Glory. What a concept!

I admit I need to be reminded of this fact often... This cancer, which seems so big right now, is just a pebble in the road of eternity; and I do look forward to seeing where this road is taking us. I just wish it wasn't quite so hard on Evelyn and the rest of the family as it tends to be.

I have had a pretty good couple of weeks since the last treatment, although I have had a menagerie of miscellaneous side effects; so I am quite encouraged. The 3rd treatment of 4 will be next Thursday, and the 4th one 3 weeks after that. Then all the follow-up tests will be the 2nd week in August; so we will hopefully know a lot more at that time.

On the pain side, the pump seems to be working fairly well, keeping the pain level down to very manageable, so we are very thankful for that.

I know I say it often, yet never enough: Thank you for your prayers to the Father on our behalf. I know I could not be doing what I am doing without all of your support in this way.

God's richest blessings to you and yours,
Chuck and Evelyn

Update – Sept 3 2011

A very positive answer to all of our prayers: The new drug, called Zelboraf or plx4302, did come in to Rochester this week and we were able to get it on Thursday. It is in pill form, and they are big ones! They are not quite what my dad would have called "horse pills", but that would be very close to an apt description of them. I have to take 4 of them at a time, twice a day.

Please continue to pray that this drug will work quickly to shrink the tumors. Dr. Markovic is then talking about the possibility of a quick surgery to remove the tumors if we can get them small enough to be able to do this safely. While I do not relish the thought of another surgery, this one would (I think) be welcomed. We have already scheduled another PET scan for mid- October when we can know more of what may be possible, if the Lord wants us to go this way.

Also, please continue to pray that the pain and discomfort levels would diminish with the shrinking. It is so much easier to make it through the days when this is down, even though the energy level may be down as well.

I hope each of you are enjoying the long weekend with those who are close to you. This journey has taught me again how special family and friends are. I wish I could spend time with each of you and share so much more of what God is teaching us.

Happy holiday weekend, and God's best to you,
Chuck & Evelyn

Update – August 10, 2011

It wasn't all what we wanted to hear...

First, the better news: We had the PET scan yesterday, and all the cancer is still centered in the area at the top of the left leg. It has not spread into the internal organs of the body. It does still remain in the lymph nodes.

Also, the one tumor that was fairly large in the spring has shrunk and basically gone away. This is very good news.

Second, the not-so-good news: There are two other tumors that have continued to grow, and are now about the size of golf balls in this area.

In trying to understand this, I am working to understand something much bigger than I am, I know; but I need to try anyway. This may not be the best illustration, but I think it helps me. Not all of the melanoma cells die in the same way or with the same "bullet". So we have to try different weapons. The one we have been using has done what it is able to do, and we can see this by the dead tumor; as well as by a spot on my face that is a side effect of this drug actually working. So, I am thankful for this one having worked.

Now it is time to try the next weapon: it is another new drug that targets a special gene in the melanoma, and by killing this gene, shrinks all of the cancer. No one is saying this is the next major breakthrough in cancer research, but it has shown some significant results. It is still waiting for FDA approval, but they have what is called a "compassionate usage" category for use during this time; and Dr. Markovic thinks I will qualify for this.

We are praying to this end. The drug is known as PLX 4302, and is marketed as Zelboraf.

Third, with the growth of the two tumors, has come some significant increases in the pain level. We met with the pain people yesterday as well and stepped up the dosage of pain medicine from the internal pump. It will take several days for this to kick in fully, so please pray that we have it right.

I have always tried to be a "big picture thinker". I like to see what is happening across the whole frame of things. I admit, in this case, I am having trouble seeing why God is doing this as He is; but I am reminded of the passage that says He does give us light for our path only as far as we need to see. I can trust him for the fog beyond this light. I only hope I have the strength to do this.

Thanks for praying for us, and standing behind us. We know God is good, and truly look forward to seeing how all this is going to work out.

His Best to you and yours,
Chuck & Evelyn

Update – Sept 18, 2011

Today has been one of those days when my "git up and go" got up and went without me; and did not wait for me to come along. I have felt fatigued all day.

As I mentioned last time, we did get the new drug, and were able to get it in Rochester, which was a real answer to prayer. Thanks for praying.

Another answer was that it did work from the first day to take away most of the pain around the tumors. We cannot know completely what this means until we do a PET scan in mid-October, but we are cautiously optimistic that this means it has stopped the growth of the tumors, and we will have to see if they actually begin to shrink. That is one specific prayer request.

The side effects have been a little more complicated. This drug has made me super-sensitive to the sun. After a couple of hours in the sun about the 3rd day I was on it; my cheeks started to blister, followed by my lips, and then the backs of my hands (which are still peeling 2 weeks later).

The second side effect is that it plays with my blood thinning medicine. After 2 weeks of re-adjustment after re-adjustment, we think it has finally leveled out and controlled; but it was somewhat touch and go for several days. We just did not know where the levels were going next, but the Lord is in control and I am so glad for that!

The third side effect is of some concern to us, although our oncologist doesn't seem as concerned as we are: Out of about 3,000 people who have now been started on this new drug since it was approved by the FDA about 4 weeks ago, 8 of us have developed new mole-like lesions that look like new Melanoma moles. Since this did happen to several of these 8 during the test phases, the manufacturer recommends simply removing them as soon as possible and continuing with the treatment.

Since I have several of these that have popped up in the last few days, we will go to Mayo on Tuesday to have all of them removed. Since they are so new, they should be only on the skin, not in the skin to any extent, and I understand this. It is still somewhat disconcerting to us, so I would ask you to pray for peace in this whole area for both Evelyn and myself.

We keep reminding ourselves that God is in control, and I am trying real hard to keep my emotional feet on the ground as the new drug seems to be working so well on the pain of the tumors.

He truly loves us, and we know this is a fact as we look back on all He has brought us through so far. Only He knows how much more of a journey this will be. I thank Him for the light to see one step at a time. I also thank Him for partners like yourself who stand by us and hold us up to the Throne of Grace as you do.

God bless...
Chuck and Evelyn

January 25, 2012

We have been home for several days now, and it is so nice to be here again.

We did have to make a quick trip to the emergency room the day after we came home as one of the Penrose surgical drain holes opened up. I have had to take it easy since then as we keep changing the dressings and waiting for it to heal closed. We are close to that now, and it does make me feel better.

We also have been making regular trips to Fairmont to get the blood thinners balanced. This has been a little more strenuous because of the weather and the snow/ice we have had.

The pain from this surgery has been somewhat intense, but it has gone down considerably in the last couple of days. I got a relatively good night's sleep last night, and this really helps also.

The surgeons said they were able to remove all the cancer related material they could find, along with most of the radiated tissue (skin that had been damaged by radiation). We are praying that they got all of the cancer, but we will not know this for several months as this very aggressive strain of melanoma has shown itself to be hard to get in the past. I am so grateful to know He is in control, but it is good to hear encouraging news from the surgeons as well.

I have the post op checkups with the surgeons tomorrow in Rochester (Thursday). Please pray these go well, and the healing continues. We will also meet with our oncologist next week to determine our next step as we continue to do battle with the cancer and the pain.

As I have said before, and cannot say often enough; Thank you for your prayers.

> To think in terms of a picture really only the Lord can see, but I can imagine; all of you holding Evelyn and I up before the Lord in prayer is such a great inspiration to me... thank you again.

Until I am able to write again, God Bless,
Chuck and Evelyn

February 8, 2012

We have a nice oaken clock in our living room with a great reminder for me on the face of it: It says "while we measure things in time, God measures them in Eternity." All of this pain and discomfort we go through on this earth and in this life really is part of His long-term, eternal plan. I especially need to be reminded of this when I start to ask any of the "why me..." questions...

The last 2 weeks have been really pretty good. With 34 inches of incision from this surgery, I have not had to take anything orally for pain since about the 9th or 10th day after surgery. My leg is still stiff, and I do feel that, but I can generally work out some of the stiffness by walking around the house a little bit. I'm not too good at stairs yet, though.

The other challenge we have right now is for the new skin to be healing to the old, somewhat radiated skin. There is still some seepage coming through one area (about an inch) of where these come together. I have to try to keep this as clean as possible and change the dressing on it often.

Please pray for the stiffness and the seepage issues. The thing I am most concerned with is getting some infection through the seepage area.

We go back to see the surgeon next Monday, the 13th, to have at least some of the stitches removed. After all the stitches are able to be removed, we will have another PET scan done to give us a post-surgery baseline to use in determining what next steps to take.

Thanks for all your prayers and support.

Blessings...
Chuck and Ev

February 17, 2012

Today would have been both my Dad's (94th) and my Grandma Hallstrom's (114th I think) birthday. They both meant a lot to me (and still do). I am so grateful to the Lord for the Godly heritage I have had from many in my ancestral lines. I also know how much of a responsibility it is to pass this along to my children, grandchildren and others.

I guess if you have never thought about this, and even if you don't have this kind of heritage, let me offer a thought: If you don't have this, then start it with your own children and grandchildren... and others you know in your circle of influence. Heaven will be a lot more fun if you do this.

When we saw the surgeon on Monday, he took all the stitches out. We still have a little seepage, but as long as I keep it clean, he said he is not concerned and it should heal itself in a couple of weeks. That is what we are hoping and praying for at this point.

The stiffness of the muscles that were moved from the abdomen to the leg is also of concern. As the surgeon said, "These muscles do not know what to do down there in the leg and must be retrained...". At this point they are not retrained and they are very stiff and uncomfortable.

We are planning a PET scan for March 5. This will give a baseline for watching for the melanoma to come back. We are praying that the surgeons got it all this time, and that the journey may be winding down for us. Only the Lord knows what is ahead, and I pray I am strong enough to take it one step at a time.

Your support and prayers have sustained us to this point, and I am so grateful you have been part of this with us.

God bless,
Chuck & Evelyn

Chuck Rudolph

June 20, 2012

I am finally home (have been for about two weeks), but am still very weak. I walked about a half block today and needed to rest. At least the pain has been greatly reduced. There is always some discomfort, but this is manageable for the time being.

I want to thank all of you who called, and/or sent messages or cards of encouragement while I was in the hospital for the 5 & ½ weeks. Also, a big thank you to those who sent gas money for Ev to be able to be with me in Rochester often. And then there are those of you who have provided meals and other services (like mowing the lawn and changing the oil in the pickup). I cannot thank you enough! Only God knows how special this is to us.

A request: For whatever reason, both of my heels are very tender and sore. This makes walking very difficult. Please pray that this will be alleviated soon.

We go tomorrow to Rochester again for a consultation with the oncologist about what comes next. I know the Lord will be guiding, but I do admit that the journey is getting to be much longer than we had thought it could... We do need you to keep lifting us up to the Throne of Grace. God is good.

Thank you again for your support.

Blessings to you and yours,
Chuck and Ev

Family and Close Friends

May I speak to you who are family and close friends of someone going through perilous times?

There is nothing inherently right or wrong about the feelings you had and how you did or did not express them immediately when you heard the news. We all are different, and we will see times like these in very diverse ways; different maybe in extreme ways. But none of these feelings are made of black and white material.

What is important is not how we felt then, but where you go from there. Maybe you feel guilty at what you said or thought, and that you could never get by this. Maybe you are bitter at hearing the news and having to immediately become a caregiver in ways that affect your own life or lifestyle.

However you felt then really doesn't matter. What does matter is that Jesus wants to be glorified in this entire situation, and especially in your life.

Let me urge you to look to Jesus. He is the author of all life, and as you are looking to Him, He will draw you closer to Himself.

To begin a relationship with Jesus is really quite simple: just thank Him for dying on the cross of Calvary to take away your sin; and thank Him for coming out of the grave, conquering death so that you can have New Life with Him, now and forever.

After this, just ask Him to show you what to do (recognizing he may only show you one step at a time).

Then, find a Bible-believing church and attend it regularly. We all need people around us who love Jesus and want to help us grow in our trusting of Him.

About the Authors

Chuck and Evelyn Rudolph

Chuck Rudolph grew up in rural southern Minnesota. He spent many years working with Youth for Christ.

In 2008 he was diagnosed with Melanoma cancer. He was classified stage 4 for 3 1/2 years. In 2012, his family was told he would not leave the hospital alive; but by God's grace, he was healed and enjoys telling his story of what God has done in his life.

Evelyn Rudolph also grew up in rural southern Minnesota. She and Chuck went to school together. She also has worked with Youth for Christ in many capacities and continues working with YFC in Martin County, Minnesota where they reside. They have been married for 46+ years.

Meloni Rudolph

Meloni Rudolph is the daughter of Chuck and Evelyn. She is currently the Dean of Student Life at the Community College of Denver. During her career she has worked at several colleges and universities; and has twice sailed as part of the staff of Semester at Sea.

Meloni and her fiancé (Tony Crawford) are planning a wedding for June of 2015.

Please let us know if this book has been helpful
to you. You may reach us by email:

Ajourneythroughcancer@gmail.com

Chuck Rudolph is available for speaking engagements
and for 4—6 hour seminars to help your church be
better equipped to care for the sick, elderly and shut-
ins. Please contact him at the above address.

Printed in the United States
By Bookmasters